Keto Cravings

60 decadent keto and low carb recipes to satisfy your sweet tooth!

disclaimer.

© Copyright Kalie Stephan, September 2018. All rights reserved,

No part of this publication should be reproduced or distributed in any form or by any means, electronic or mechanical or stored in a database without prior permission from the publisher.

Book cover & illustrations by Kalie Stephan.

Kalie Stephan, aka 'The Hungry Elephant' is NOT a medical doctor and does not hold any responsibility for any medical conditions that are believed to be linked to the food intake. Please see the doctor before you make any big changes to the diet.

More information on the keto diet and delicious recipes can be found at www.hungryelephant.ca

ISBN: 9781796987430

Published Independently

Elements used in nutritional information graphics are in part created by Brusheezy Brushes at Brusheezy.com

about the author.

Kalie Stephan is a former TV writer and producer with a passion for cooking. Born in Canada, she currently is living in southern Ireland.

In February of 2017, she started living a ketogenic life, eliminating carbohydrates and sugar from her diet. In a span of 5 months, she lost nearly 50 pounds and has seen a drastic improvement in her mental health.

notes.

The white sugar substitutes used in this cookbook is an erythritol/monk fruit mix. Lakanto is a good brand, however if you can't find an erythritol/monk fruit mix, you can also use plain erythritol such as Swerve.

Please note, if you use pure Stevia, you will have to use significantly less than what the recipe calls for.

The brown sugar substitute used in these recipes is an erythritol/stevia mix by Sukrin Gold. Lakanto & Swerve also produce decent brown sugar substitutes.

All nutritional information is PER SERVING unless stated otherwise.

Videos for these recipes can be found at **hungryelephant.ca** or **youtube.com/hungryelephant**

contents.

6. CAKES.

34. PIES & CHEESECAKE.

59. CUPCAKES, MUFFINS & BREAD.

86. COOKIES.

108. MORE SWEETS & TREATS.

136. BAKING TIPS.

CAKES.

contents.

BUTTER CAKE	9
STRAWBERRY SHORTCAKE	10
BOSTON CREAM POKE CAKE	13
CHOCOLATE CAKE WITH PEANUT BUTTER ICING	14
BIRTHDAY CAKE	17
COFFEE CAKE	28
CHOCOLATE CAKE WITH CARAMEL DRIZZLE	21
BOURBON CHOCOLATE CAKE	22
PUMPKIN SPICE CAKE	25
BLACK FOREST CAKE (LOW CARB)	26
TIRAMISU CAKE	29
LEMON CAKE	30
CHOCOFLAN	33

KENTUCKY BUTTER CAKE

Serves: 12

CAKE

- 2 cups (230g) almond flour - packed
- 1/2 cup (115g) sour cream
- 1/2 cup (100g) butter
- 3 eggs
- 2/3 cup (120g) sugar substitute
- 1 tsp baking powder
- 1 tsp vanilla

SYRUP

- 1/4 cup (50g) butter
- 1/3 cup (60g) sugar substitute
- 1 tbsp vanilla
- 2 tbsp water

1. In a mixing bowl, whisk together the cake ingredients.
2. Pour the batter into a greased bundt pan.
3. Bake at 350°F / 175°C for 35 minutes.
4. Let cake cool inside bundt pan.
5. Melt butter in a pot over medium heat.
6. Whisk in the sugar substitute, vanilla and water. Heat until it the sugar substitute has dissolved and take off heat.
7. Use a skewer or a round end of a utensil to poke several holes into the top (technically bottom) of the bundt cake.
8. Pour butter mixture onto the cake, making sure the holes evenly fill with the syrup.
9. Cool for 1 hour.
10. Flip cake out of the bundt pan and serve!

 266 kcal
 25.8 fat
 5.4 carbs
 2 fibre
 3.4 net
 6.2 protein

STRAWBERRY SHORT CAKE

Serves: 12

CAKE

- 1/2 cup (120g) sour cream
- 1/2 cup (118ml) water
- 1/2 cup (100g) sugar substitute
- 1/2 cup (50g) butter – melted
- 2 eggs
- 2 cups (180g) almond flour
- 1 tsp baking powder
- 1 1/2 cups halved strawberries
- tsp vanilla

CREAM

- 2 cups (500ml) heavy cream
- 1/2 cup (100g) sugar substitute
- tbsp vanilla

1. In a mixing bowl, whisk together the cake ingredients.
2. Halve the batter into two 9-inch cake pans lined with parchment paper.
3. Bake at 350°F / 175°C for 25 minutes.
4. Use a hand or stand mixer to whip the heavy cream, sugar substitute and vanilla to stiff peaks.
5. Place one cake on a stand and top with half the whipped cream, spreading evenly.
6. Add a layer of strawberries.
7. Place the second cake on top.
8. Top with the rest of the whipped cream and strawberries.
9. Serve!

 291 kcal
 27.7 fat
 7.3 carbs
 2.4 fibre
 4.9 net
 6.3 protein

BOSTON CREAM POKE CAKE

Serves: 10

CAKE

- 1/4 cup (50g) sour cream
- 1/4 cup (59ml) water
- 1 tsp vanilla
- 1 egg
- 1/4 cup (57g) sugar substitute
- 50g melted butter
- 1 1/4 cup (120g) almond flour
- 1/2 tsp baking powder

CUSTARD

- 1 cup (250ml) heavy cream
- 1 tsp vanilla
- 3 tbsp sugar substitute
- 3 egg yolks
- 1/4 tsp xanthan gum

+ 1 sugar free chocolate bar! (approx 40g)

1. In a mixing bowl, whisk together the cake ingredients.

2. Pour into a 6-inch cake pan lined with parchment paper or greased with butter.

3. Bake at 350°F / 175°C for 25 minutes.

4. Bring the heavy cream to a light boil on medium heat,

5. In a separate bowl, whisk together the egg yolks and sugar substitute.

6. Once the cream is at a boil, pour half into the egg yolks, while whisking.

7. Pour the cream/yolk mixture back into the rest of the cream and stir continuously. It should thicken.

9. Take off heat and whisk in vanilla & xanthan gum.

10. Use a skewer or circular utensil to poke several holes in the cake.

11. Pour the custard on top of the cake and spread evenly.

12. Chill for 3-4 hours in the fridge.

13. Once ready to serve, melt chocolate in microwave and pour on top of the cake.

 237 kcal
 22.7 fat
 6.3 carbs
 1.9 fibre
 4.4 net
 4.7 protein

CHOCOLATE CAKE WITH
peanut butter icing

Serves: 10

CAKE

- 1/2 cup sour cream
- 4 tbsp black cocoa
- 2 tbsp regular cocoa
- 1/4 cup water (59ml)
- 1/2 cup (100g) butter – melted
- 1/3 (66g) cup sugar substitute
- 2 eggs
- 2 cups (200g) almond flour
- 1 tsp baking powder
- 2 tbsp vinegar

ICING

- 8oz Cream Cheese
- 5 tbsp sugar substitute
- 1 tsp vanilla extract
- 1/2 cup (67g) sugar free peanut butter

1. In a mixing bowl, whisk together the cake ingredients.

2. Separate batter into two 7-inch cake pans, greased or lined with parchment paper.

3. Bake at 350°F / 175°C for 35-40 minutes.

4. Let cakes cool to room temperature.

5. Using a hand or stand mixer, blend icing ingredients until thoroughly combined.

6. Place a few dollops of icing onto one of the cakes and spread around.

7. Place the second cake on top and continue icing the cake.

8. Serve and enjoy!

 320 kcal
 29.1 fat
 8.1 carbs
 3.2 fibre
 4.9 net
 9.6 protein

BIRTHDAY CAKE

Serves: 10

SPRINKLES:
- 4 tbsp unsweetened coconut
- Liquid food colouring

CAKE:
- 1/2 cup (100g) sour cream
- 1 tsp vanilla
- 1/3 cup (78ml) water
- 5 tbsp sugar substitute
- 1/2 cup (100g) melted butter
- 3 eggs
- 2 cups (200g) almond flour
- 1 tsp baking powder

ICING:
- 16oz cream cheese (2 bricks)
- 4 oz cacao butter
- 6 1/2 tbsp powered sweetener
- 1 tsp vanilla

1. Separate the coconut flakes into 4 bowls.

2. Stir in a drop or two of food colouring to each bowl.

3. Coat coconut flakes evenly and set aside to let dry.

4. In a mixing bowl, whisk together the cake ingredients and stir in some of the 'sprinkles'.

5. Separate batter into two 7-inch cake pans, greased or lined with parchment paper.

6. Bake at 350°F / 175°C for 35-40 minutes.

7. Using a hand or stand mixer, blend icing ingredients until thoroughly combined.

6. Place a few dollops of icing onto one of the cakes and spread around.

8. Place the second cake on top and continue icing the cake.

9. Top with the sprinkles!

 425 kcal
 40.6 fat
 6.3 carbs
 2.3 fibre
 4 net
 8.7 protein

COFFEE CAKE

Serves: 8

CAKE

- 1/2 cup (100g) sour cream
- 1/3 cup (78ml) brewed coffee
- 1/2 cup (100g) butter - melted
- 3 eggs
- 1/2 cup sugar substitute
- 2 1/4 (220g) cup almond flour
- 1 tsp baking powder

SYRUP:

- 1/3 cup (78ml) water
- 5 tbsp sugar substitute
- 1/2 tsp instant coffee

1. In a mixing bowl, whisk together the cake ingredients.

2. Pour the batter into a bundt cake pan.

3. Bake at 350°F / 175°C for 35-40 minutes.

4. Let cool to room temperature.

5. Stir together the syrup ingredients in a small pan on medium heat.

6. Continue to heat until the sugar substitute dissolves.

7. Pour onto the cake.

8. Serve and enjoy!!

307 kcal | 28.9 fat | 6.8 carbs | 3 fibre | 3.8 net | 8.9 protein

CHOCOLATE CAKE with a caramel drizzle

Serves: 10

CAKE:

- 1/2 cup (100g) sour cream
- 5 tbsp cocoa
- 1 cup (236ml) water
- 1/4 cup (50g) butter - melted
- 1/2 cup (100g) sugar substitute
- 3 eggs
- 2 cups (200g) almond flour
- 1 tsp baking powder

DRIZZLE

- 2 tbsp erythritol
- 1 tbsp butter
- 1 tbsp heavy cream
- Sea salt (optional)

1. In a mixing bowl, whisk together the cake ingredients.

2. Pour the batter into a greased bundt pan.

3. Bake at 350°F / 175°C for 35 minutes.

4. Let cake cool inside bundt pan.

5. Melt erythritol in a deep pan over medium heat.

6. Add in butter and cream. It will start to bubble.

7. Stir frequently to avoid burning.

8. Once it becomes a dark amber colour, take off heat.

9. Pour on the cake and top with sea salt if wanted.

220 kcal | 19.3 fat | 6.9 carbs | 2.9 fibre | 4 net | 7.6 protein

BOURBON CHOCOLATE TORTE

Serves: 12

CAKE

- 1/2 cup (120g) sour cream
- 1/2 cup (118ml) bourbon
- 1/4 cup (50g) butter – melted
- 3 eggs – beaten
- 2 cups (200g) almond flour
- 1 tsp baking powder
- 3 tbsp dark cocoa powder
- 2 tbsp regular cocoa powder
- 1/2 cup (100g) sugar substitute

GANACHE:

- 2 keto, sugar free, chocolate bars (approx 150g total)
- 4 tbsp bourbon

1. In a mixing bowl, whisk together the cake ingredients.

2. Pour the batter into a 9-inch cake pan.

3. Bake at 350°F / 175°C for 30 minutes.

4. Let cool to room temperature.

5. In a pot on medium heat, melt the chocolate and bourbon, stirring frequently.

6. Once the chocolate is smooth and shiny, take off heat.

7. Pour the ganache over the cake and use a spatula to spread it evenly around the cake.

8. Serve and enjoy!

 268 kcal
 21.3 fat
 6.7 carbs
 3.2 fibre
 3.5 net
 7.2 protein

PUMPKIN SPICE CAKE

Serves: 10

CAKE

- 2/3 cup (140g) pumpkin puree
- 1/2 cup (100g) butter – melted
- 1/2 cup (118ml) water
- 1 tbsp cinnamon
- 1/2 tsp nutmeg
- 1/2 tsp allspice
- 1/4 cup (50g) sugar substitute
- 3 eggs
- 2 cups (200g) almond flour
- 1 tsp baking powder

ICING:

- 1 pkg (250g) cream cheese
- 1/4 cup (40g) powdered sugar substitute
- 1 tsp vanilla

1. In a mixing bowl, whisk together the cake ingredients.

2. Separate the batter into two 7-inch cake pan.

3. Bake at 350°F / 175°C for 30 minutes.

4. Let cool to room temperature.

5. Use a hand or stand mixer to whip the cream cheese, sugar substitute and vanilla.

6. Place a dollop of icing onto of one of the cakes and spread evenly around.

7. Carefully drop the second cake on top of the icing.

8. Use the rest of the icing to spread evenly around the cake.

9. Enjoy!

 306 kcal
 27.9 fat
 6.6 carbs
 2.7 fibre
 3.9 net
 9.8 protein

LOW CARB BLACK FOREST CAKE

Serves: 10

CAKE

- 1/2 cup (115g) sour cream
- 3 tbsp dark cocoa powder
- 2 tbsp regular cocoa powder
- 1/4 cup (60ml) water
- 1/4 cup (50g) sugar substitute
- 1/2 cup (100g) melted butter
- 2 eggs
- 2 cups (200g) almond flour
- 1 tsp baking powder

ICING:

- 1/2 cup (125ml) heavy cream
- 1/4 cup (50g) sugar substitute
- 1 tbsp vanilla
- 1 tub (250g) mascarpone cheese
- 3/4 cup (100g) cherries – pitted
- Sugar free chocolate sauce

1. In a mixing bowl, whisk together the cake ingredients.

2. Separate the batter into two 6-inch cake pan.

3. Bake at 350°F / 175°C for 30 minutes.

4. Let cool to room temperature.

5. Use a hand or stand mixer to whip the heavy cream, sugar substitute and vanilla.

6. Slowly mix in the mascarpone cheese.

7. Place one cake on a stand and top with half the whipped cream, spreading evenly.

7. Add a layer of cherries.

8. Place the second cake on top.

9. Top with the rest of the whipped cream, cherries and sugar free chocolate sauce.

332 kcal | 32.2 fat | 8 carbs | 3 fibre | 5 net | 6.9 protein

TIRAMISU CAKE

Serves: 12

CAKE

- 1/2 cup (115g) sour cream
- 1 teaspoon vanilla
- 1/2 cup (65g) butter – melted
- 1/3 cup (78ml) brewed coffee
- 1/2 cup (100g) sugar substitute
- 3 eggs
- 2 cups (200g) almond flour
- 1 tsp baking powder

ICING:

- 1 1/8th cup (250g) mascarpone cheese
- 1 cup (236ml) heavy cream – whipped
- 1/2 cup (100g) sugar substitute
- 1 tbsp vanilla

1. In a mixing bowl, whisk together the cake ingredients.

2. Separate the batter into two 7-inch cake pan.

3. Bake at 350°F / 175°C for 30 minutes.

4. Let cool to room temperature.

5. Use a hand or stand mixer to whip the heavy cream, sugar substitute and vanilla.

7. Fold in the mascarpone cheese.

6. Place a dollop of icing onto of one of the cakes and spread evenly around.

7. Carefully drop the second cake on top of the icing.

8. Use the rest of the icing to spread evenly around the cake.

9. Sprinkle some cocoa powder on top!

 323 kcal
 31.5 fat
 6.6 carbs
 4 fibre
 2.6 net
 6.1 protein

TART LEMON POPPYSEED CAKE

Serves: 10

CAKE

- 1/2 cup (100g) sour cream
- 1/4 cup (60ml) lemon juice
- 1/3 cup (46g) sugar substitute
- 3 eggs
- 2 cups (200g) almond flour
- 1 tbsp poppy seeds
- 1 tsp baking soda
- additional 2 tbsp lemon juice

ICING:

- 1/2 cup (70g) powdered sugar substitute
- 2-3 tbsp lemon juice

1. In a mixing bowl, whisk together the cake ingredients.

2. Pour the batter into a bundt cake.

3. Bake at 350°F / 175°C for 40 minutes.

4. Let cool to room temperature.

5. In a small mixing bowl, whisk together the sugar substitute and lemon juice. If this is too tart - add a few tbsp of heavy cream.

6. Pour the glaze over the cake.

7. Optional - top with crushed almonds!

8. Serve and enjoy!

 175 kcal
 15 fat
 5.7 carbs
 2.5 fibre
 3.2 net
 7.1 protein

Chocoflan

Serves: 12

CAKE:
- 1 1/2 cups (150g) almond flour
- 1/2 cup (45g) chocolate protein powder
- 2 tbsp cocoa powder
- 1/4 cup (50g) sugar substitute
- 1 tsp baking powder
- 1/4 cup (60g) sour cream
- 2 eggs
- 1/2 cup (117ml) water
- 1/4 cup (50g) butter - melted

FLAN:
- 2 cups (500ml) heavy cream
- 4 eggs
- 2/3 cup (125g) sugar substitute
- 1 tbsp vanilla extract

OTHER:
- sugar free caramel sauce or cajeta
- butter for greasing
- hot water

1. In a mixing bowl, whisk together all the ingredients for the cake.
2. In another bowl, mix together the flan ingredients.
3. Place a thin layer of caramel sauce/cajeta on the bottom of the greased bundt pan.
4. Pour in the cake batter.
5. Pour in the flan mixture on top of the cake.
6. Place the bundt pan into a casserole dish and pour 1-inch of boiling water into the casserole dish.
7. Cover the bundt pan tightly with foil & bake at 350°F / 176°C for 70-80 minutes.
8. Cool to room temp before serving.

 309 kcal
 28.9 fat
 5.4 carbs
 1.8 fibre
 3.6 net
 9.8 protein

pies. & cheesecake.

contents.

PECAN PIE	36
MISSISSIPPI MUD PIE	39
BANANA CREAM PIE	40
PUMPKIN PIE	43
MINI 'APPLE' PIES	44
SWIRL CHEESECAKE	47
JAPANESE CHEESECAKE	48
CANDIED PECAN CHEESECAKE	51
PUMPKIN CHEESECAKE	52
ICE CREAM CHEESECAKE	55
RASPBERRY CHEESECAKE	56

PECAN PIE

Serves: 10

CRUST:

- 4 tbsp butter – room temp
- 1 tsp vanilla
- 3 tbsp sugar substitute
- 1 cup (100g) almond flour

FILLING:

- 2 eggs - beaten
- 3/4 cup (135g) brown sugar substitute
- 1/4 cup (50g) sugar substitute
- 1 tsp vanilla
- 1/8th cup (30ml) maple syrup
- 2 tbsp butter – melted
- 3 tbsp almond flour
- 1 1/2 cups (150g) chopped pecans

1. In a mixing bowl, use a spatula to cream the butter, vanilla and sugar substitute together.

2. Pour in the almond flour and knead together with the hands until a dough forms.

3. Spread the dough onto an 8-inch non-stick pie pan to form a crust.

4. Poke several times with a fork and bake at 350°F / 175°C for 10 minutes.

5. Take out and pour the pecans into the crust.

6. In a mixing bowl, whisk together the filling ingredients (minus the pecans).

7. Pour the filling into the pie crust.

8. Cover with foil and bake at 350°F / 175°C for 30 minutes.

 258 kcal
 25.8 fat
 4.8 carbs
 2.8 fibre
 2 net
 5.3 protein

MISSISSIPPI MUD PIE

Serves: 15

1st LAYER:

- 1/2 cup (100g) butter
- 5 tbsp cocoa
- 1/4 cup (50g) sugar substitute
- 1 egg - beaten
- 1 cup (100g) almond flour
- 1 cup (75g) unsweetened coconut flakes

2nd LAYER:

- 2 cups (500ml) heavy cream
- 1/2 cup (100g) sugar substitute
- 3 egg yolks - beaten
- 5 tbsp cocoa
- 1/4 tsp xanthan gum

3rd LAYER:

- 1 cup (250ml) heavy cream
- 1/4 cup (50g) sugar substitute
- tsp vanilla

1. Whisk together the butter, sugar substitute and cocoa in a pan on medium heat.

2. Turn the heat down to low and slowly stir in the beaten egg.

3. Take off heat and immediately stir in the almond flour and coconut flakes until a dough forms.

4. Spread the mixture to cover the bottom of a 8x10 casserole dish. Let it cool.

5. For the second layer, whisk together the heavy cream and cocoa powder and bring to a low boil on medium heat.

6. Take off heat and slowly pour in the egg yolks, stirring the cream as you pour.

7. Put the pan back on the heat and whisk in the sugar substitute and xanthan gum.

8. Cook for an additional 5 minutes, stirring frequently until the custard thickens up.

9. Pour on top of the first layer and cool.

10. Finally, use a hand or stand mixer to whip up the 3rd layer ingredients to stiff peaks.

11. Spread the whipped cream over top of the second layer and sprinkle with cocoa powder.

12. Serve.

 201 kcal
 17.5 fat
 9.6 carbs
 2.7 fibre
 6.9 net
 4.2 protein

BANANA CREAM PIE

Serves: 10

CRUST:

- 3/4 cup (90g) coconut flour
- 1/2 cup (65g) butter – melted
- 2 eggs
- 3 tbsp sugar substitute

FILLING:

- 1 cup (250ml) heavy cream
- 3 egg yolks - beaten
- 3 tbsp sugar substitute
- 1 tsp banana flavouring
- 1/2 tsp vanilla extract
- 1/2 tsp xanthan gum

1. In a mixing bowl, whisk together the melted butter, eggs and sugar substitute.

2. Slowly stir in the coconut flour until a dough forms.

3. Spread the dough out evenly in a 6-inch pie pan.

4. Poke several holes into the pie with a fork and bake for 10 minutes at 350°F / 175°C.

5. Bring the heavy cream to a low boil.

6. Take off heat and slowly pour in the beaten egg yolks, whisking the cream as you pour.

7. Put the cream back on medium-low, and stir in the banana flavouring, vanilla extract, sugar substitute and xanthan gum.

8. Once the custard starts to thicken up, pour it into the pie crust.

9. Cover and refrigerate minimum 4 hours but ideally overnight.

196 kcal | 17.6 fat | 5.7 carbs | 3 fibre | 2.7 net | 3.8 protein

Crustless Pumpkin Pie

Serves: 12

PIE:

- 1 can (3 1/4 cups/800g) pumpkin puree
- 1 cup (200g) white sugar substitute
- 1/2 cup (90g) brown sugar substitute
- 2 tbsp cinnamon
- 1 tbsp nutmeg
- 1 tsp ginger
- 1 tsp ground cloves
- 1 1/2 cups (355ml) heavy cream
- 4 eggs
- Salt

PECANS:

- 3/4 cup (70g) chopped pecans
- 3 tbsp water
- 1/4 cup (50g) white sugar substitute
- 1/4 cup (45g) brown sugar substitute
- 1 tsp cinnamon

1. Pre-heat oven to 425°F/220°C.

2. In a mixing bowl, whisk all the pie ingredients together thoroughly.

3. Pour into a 9-inch cake or pie dish, lined with parchment paper.

4. Place in the oven and immediately turn the oven down to 350°F/175°C and cook for 1 hour.

*You will know when the pie is done when it does NOT jiggle when tapping the sides of the pan with a fork, or giving it a quick wiggle.

5. Take out and let cool.

6. Melt the sugar substitutes in a pan over medium heat, along with the cinnamon and water. Bring to a boil.

7. Pour in the pecans and cook until the water has boiled off. Stir frequently

8. Scoop the pecans on top of the pie and let cool.

9. Serve with some whipped cream!

202 kcal | 18.8 fat | 6.3 carbs | 2 fibre | 4.3 net | 3.9 protein

MINI 'APPLE' PIES

Serves: 6

CRUST:

- 1 1/2 cups (170g) mozzarella
- 3/4 cup (86g) almond flour
- 2 tbsp cream cheese
- 1/2 tsp baking powder
- 1/8th tsp xanthan gum
- 1/2 tbsp cinnamon
- 1/4 tsp nutmeg
- 1 egg

FILLING:

- 2 tbsp butter
- 1 1/2 tbsp cinnamon
- 1/4 tsp nutmeg
- 1/4 tsp ginger
- 2 zucchini – peeled & chopped
- 2 tbsp water
- 1/3 cup (70g) sugar substitute
- 1/4 tsp xanthan gum

1. To make the crust - melt the mozzarella and almond flour cheese in the microwave, using a microwavable safe bowl.

2. Stir in the almond flour, baking powder, cinnamon nutmeg and egg. Knead with the hands until a sticky dough forms.

3. Roll the dough flat between two pieces of parchment paper

4. Take some dough and line the cups of a muffin tin. Set aside.

5. Melt the butter in a non-stick pan on medium heat.

6. Whisk in the cinnamon, nutmeg, ginger, water, sugar substitute and xanthan gum.

7. Pour in the chopped zucchini and stir to coat evenly.

8. Cook for an additional 4-5 minutes.

9. Take off heat and let cool.

10. Scoop the zucchini filling into the cups.

11. Bake at 350°F / 175°C for 30 minutes.

223 kcal | 18 fat | 6.5 carbs | 2.7 fibre | 3.8 net | 10.7 protein

Swirl Cheesecake

Serves: 10

CRUST:

- 3/4 cup (90g) coconut flour
- 1/2 cup (65g) butter - melted
- 2 eggs
- 3 tbsp sugar substitute
- 1 tsp cinnamon

FILLING:

- 2 cups (500g) cream cheese
- 1 tbsp vanilla
- 1/2 cup (100g) sugar substitute
- 1/2 cup (100g) sour cream
- 2 eggs
- 3 tbsp almond flour
- 2 tbsp heavy cream
- 2 1/2 tbsp cocoa powder

1. In a mixing bowl, stir together the coconut flour, cinnamon, eggs, sugar substitute and melted butter.
2. Spread the crust to cover a lined or greased 9-inch spring form cake pan.
3. In a mixing bowl, whisk together all the filling ingredients except the cocoa powder & heavy cream.
4. Take a small portion of the filling and put it into a separate bowl.
5. In the smaller bowl, mix in the cocoa powder and heavy cream.
6. Pour the vanilla cheesecake mix into the cake pan.
7. Top with the chocolate cheesecake mix and use a spoon to combine & swirl the two mixes together.
8. Bake at 350°F / 176°F for 10 minutes, then 40 minutes at 200°F / 100°C

223 kcal | 19.8 fat | 5.1 carbs | 2.1 fibre | 3 net | 4.8 protein

Japanese Cheesecake

Serves: 10

INGREDIENTS:

- 1 tbsp powdered sweetener
- 125g (1/2 cup) cream cheese
- 1 cup (250ml) heavy cream
- 3 eggs, separated
- 1 tbsp vanilla extract
- 1/4 cup (30g) coconut flour
- 1/2 tbsp baking powder
- 1 tbsp vinegar
- 1/4 cup (35g) powdered sweetener

1. Pre-heat the oven to 350°F / 175°C.
2. In a double boiler, melt the cream cheese and mix with the cream and tbsp of powdered sweetener.
3. Take it off the heat and cool for 5 minutes.
4. Whisk the cream cheese mixture & vanilla into the egg yolks.
5. Sift the coconut flour and baking powder into the cream cheese mix and whisk thoroughly.
6. In a clean bowl, beat the egg whites and vinegar until the whites are bubbly.
7. Slowly add in the 1/4 cup of powdered sugar while you beat the whites to STIFF peaks.
8. Slowly fold small portions of the egg whites into the cream cheese mixture.
9. Place into a cake dish that is either lined with parchment paper or greased.
10. Place that cake dish into another larger cake dish and fill that with HOT water (a water bath)
11. Place both dishes in the oven and immediately turn the temp to 320°F / 160°C and bake for 40 minutes.
12. Turn the oven down to 300°F / 150°C and let it cook for an additional 30 minutes.
13. Cool in oven for 15 mins, then 4hrs in fridge before serving.

 163 kcal
 14.6 fat
 3 carbs
 1 fibre
 2 net
 3.6 protein

Candied Pecan Cheesecake

Serves: 12

CRUST:
- 1/2 cup (60g) coconut flour
- 1/4 cup (50g) butter – melted
- 1 egg
- 2 tbsp sugar substitute
- 1 tbsp cinnamon

FILLING:
- 2 cups (500g) cream cheese
- 1 tbsp vanilla
- 1/2 cup (100g) sugar substitute
- 1/2 cup (100g) sour cream
- 2 eggs
- 1 1/2 tbsp coconut flour
- 1 1/4 cups (150g) pecans – chopped
- 3 tbsp water
- 3 tbsp erythritol
- 1 tbsp brown sugar substitute

1. In a mixing bowl, whisk together the crust ingredients.
2. Spread the dough around the bottom of a 9-inch pie pan to form a crust.
3. Bake at 350°F/175°C for 10 minutes. Take out and set aside.
4. Use a hand or stand mixer to thoroughly whisk together the cream cheese, sour cream, vanilla, 1/2 cup of sugar substitute, coconut flour and eggs. Set aside.
5. In a non-stick pan on medium heat, bring the water, brown sugar substitute and 3 tbsp of erythritol to a boil.
6. Pour in the chopped pecans and continue to cook on medium heat until all the water cooks off.
7. Incorporate 3/4 of the candied pecans into the cheesecake batter.
8. Bake 350°F/175°C for 10 minutes then turn down the heat to 200°F/100°C and bake for an hour. Top with leftover pecans.

 285 kcal
 25.5 fat
 6.6 carbs
 3.3 fibre
 3.3 net
 6.4 protein

Pumpkin Cheesecake

Serves: 4

INGREDIENTS:

- 1/4 cup (55g) pumpkin puree
- 1/4 cup (50g) sour cream
- 1 tbsp cinnamon
- 1 tsp nutmeg
- 1 tsp allspice
- 1 tsp vanilla
- 1 egg
- 1 cup (250g) cream cheese
- 1/4 cup (50g) sugar substitute
- 1 tbsp almond flour

1. Place ALL the ingredients into a mixing bowl.
2. Use a hand or stand mixer to thoroughly beat all the ingredients together.
3. Pour the batter into 4 ramekins.
4. Bake at 350°F/175°C for 10 minutes, then turn the oven down to 200°F/95°C for 45 minutes.
5. Turn the oven off and leave the door slightly ajar, cooling the cheesecakes.

You will know the cake is done when it is slightly jiggly in the centre but firm towards the outside.

**If you want to bake this as one entire cake, use the same time & temp, but check after 45 minutes.*

148 kcal | 13.1 fat | 4.6 carbs | 1 fibre | 3.6 net | 3.9 protein

Ice Cream Cheesecake

Serves: 10

CRUST:
- 1 cup (100g) almond flour
- 1 heaping tbsp nutmeg
- 2 tbsp cinnamon
- 3 tbsp melted butter

CAKE:
- 1 cup (236ml) heavy cream
- 1 brick (250g) cream cheese
- 3/4 cup (150g) sugar substitute
- 1 tbsp vanilla

1. In a bowl, mix together the almond flour, nutmeg and cinnamon.
2. Add in the butter and mix thoroughly. The almond flour will look darker and stick together easily if you press together.
3. Pour the almond flour mix into a spring form cake pan. Press it down flat over the bottom of the pan.
4. In another mixing bowl, whip the heavy cream until soft peaks form.
5. Mix in the cream cheese, sugar substitute and vanilla.
6. Blend together and pour the mixture into the cake pan.
7. Freeze for at least 4 hours before serving.

 223 kcal
 19.8 fat
 5.1 carbs
 2.1 fibre
 3 net
 4.8 protein

Raspberry Cheesecake for Two

Serves: 4

CRUST:
- 2 tbsp almond flour
- 1/2 tbsp cocoa powder
- 1 tbsp sugar substitute
- 1 tbsp butter - melted

CAKE:
- 1 cup (130g) cream cheese
- 1/4 cup (50g) sour cream
- 1 medium egg
- 1 tsp vanilla
- 1/4 cup (90g) sugar substitute
- 4 tbsp almond flour

JAM:
- 2/3 cup (100g) raspberries
- 2 tbsp sugar substitute
- 4 tbsp water
- 1/2 tsp xanthan gum

1. In a pot over medium heat, bring the jam ingredients to a low boil.
2. Use a fork to mash the raspberries.
3. Take off heat and let cool
4. In a mixing bowl, whisk together the ingredients for the crust.
5. Use the batter to form an even crust along the bottom of a 4-inch cake pan. Set aside.
6. In a separate mixing bowl, whisk together the filling ingredients.
7. Pour the batter into the cake pan on top of the crust.
8. Drop spoonfuls of the raspberry sauce onto the batter and use a knife to gently swirl the sauce.
9. Bake for 15 minutes at 350°F / 176°C then at 200°F / 100°C for an additional 45 minutes.

161 kcal | 21 fat | 5.8 carbs | 1.4 fibre | 4.4 net | 9 protein

cupcakes, bread & muffins.

contents.

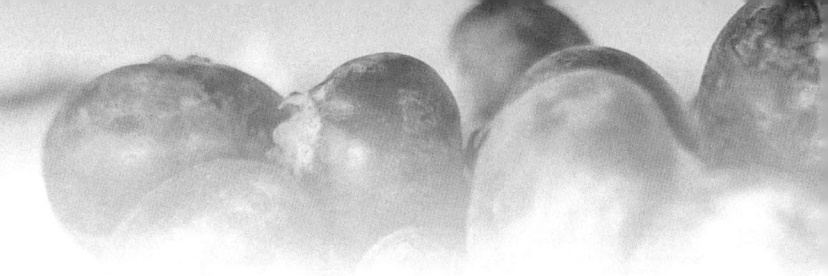

NO NUT VANILLA CUPCAKES — 60

CHOCOLATE CUPCAKES WITH COFFEE ICING — 63

RED VELVET CUPCAKES — 64

DOUBLE CHOCOLATE MUFFINS — 67

CHOCOLATE CHIP MUFFINS — 68

BLUEBERRY MUFFINS — 71

BANANA CHOCOLATE CHIP MUFFINS — 72

BANANA CHOCOLATE CHIP BREAD — 75

ALMOND SWEETBREAD — 76

CINNAMON BREAD STUFFED WITH CREAM CHEESE ICING — 79

HAWAIIAN SWEETBREAD — 80

BREAD PUDDING — 83

LEMON BREAD (STARBUCKS COPYCAT) — 84

Basic Nut Free Vanilla Cupcakes

Serves: 6

CUPCAKES:

- 1/3 cup (40g) coconut flour
- 1/4 cup (50g) sugar substitute
- 1 tsp baking powder
- 1/2 cup (125ml) heavy cream
- 2 large eggs
- 1 tsp vanilla

ICING:

- 250g mascarpone cheese
- 1 tsp vanilla
- 1/3 cup (40g) powdered sugar substitute
- 2 tbsp heavy cream

1. Whisk together the coconut flour, sugar substitute and baking powder.
2. Pour in the cream and vanilla, crack in the eggs and stir until thoroughly mixed.
3. Scoop into a muffin tin lined with cups.
4. Bake at 350°F / 175°C for 20-25 minutes or until a tooth pick comes out clean.
5. Take them out one the oven and let them cool.
6. In a mixing bowl, whisk together the mascarpone, cream, vanilla and powdered sugar substitute.
7. Use a piping tool to frost the cooled cupcakes.

 282 kcal
 26 fat
 5.1 carbs
 2.2 fibre
 2.9 net
 6.3 protein

Chocolate Cupcakes with Coffee icing

Serves: 6

CUPCAKE:

- 1/4 cup (58g) sour cream
- 2 tbsp dark cocoa powder
- 1 tbsp regular cocoa powder
- 1/4 cup (60ml) water
- 1/4 cup (50g) sugar substitute
- 1/4 cup (55g) melted butter
- 1 egg
- 1 cup (100g) almond flour
- 1/2 tsp baking powder

ICING:

- 1/2 cup (118ml) heavy cream
- 1/4 cup (50g) sugar substitute
- 1 tbsp instant coffee granules.
- 1 tub (250g) mascarpone cheese

1. Place all the cake ingredients into a mixing bowl.
2. Use a hand or stand mixer to thoroughly beat all the ingredients together.
3. Pour the batter into a muffin tin lined with muffin cups.
4. Bake at 350°F / 175°C for 25-30 minutes.
5. Take them out of the oven and let them cool.
6. While baking, beat together the icing ingredients until nice and smooth.
7. Use a piping tool to frost the cooled cupcakes.

 334 kcal
 33.2 fat
 6.3 carbs
 2.2 fibre
 4.1 net
 5.9 protein

Red Velvet Cupcakes

Serves: 6

CUPCAKES:

- 2 cups (200g) almond flour
- 2 tbsp cocoa powder
- 3 tbsp butter
- 1/3 cup (67g) sugar substitute
- 1/2 cup (100g) sour cream
- 1/3 cup (78ml) heavy cream
- 2 tsp red food colouring
- 1 tsp baking powder

ICING:

- 1/2 (100g) stick butter
- 2 tbsp mascarpone cheese
- 8 oz cream cheese
- 1/4 cup (50g) sugar substitute
- 1 tsp vanilla

1. Place all the cupcake ingredients into a mixing bowl.
2. Use a hand or stand mixer to thoroughly beat all the ingredients together.
3. Pour the batter into a muffin tin lined with muffin cups.
4. Bake at 350°F / 175°C for 25-30 minutes.
5. While baking, beat together the icing ingredients until nice and smooth.
6. Once the cupcakes are done and cooled down, cut a small hole out in the top of the cupcake.
7. Use a piping tool to frost the cooled cupcake.
8. Crumble the cupcake hole on top of the icing.

 377 kcal
 36.9 fat
 5.8 carbs
 2.3 fibre
 3.5 net
 7.7 protein

Double Chocolate Chip Muffins

Serves: 6

MUFFIN:

- 1 cup (100g) almond flour
- 1 tbsp instant coffee
- 2 1/2 tbsp cocoa powder
- 1/2 tsp baking powder
- 1/8 cup (30ml) olive oil
- 1/8 cup (30ml) heavy cream
- 1 egg
- 3 tbsp sugar substitute
- 1/2 cup (70g) sugar free chocolate chips

1. Whisk together the dry ingredients in a mixing bowl.
2. Add in the egg, extract, oil and cream.
3. Pour in the almond flour & baking powder and whisk until thoroughly mixed.
4. Stir in the chocolate chips/flakes.
5. Spoon the mix into a lined muffin tin and bake at 350°F / 175°C for roughly 25 minutes.

**At 30 minutes in, stick a toothpick into the middle of a muffin and if it comes out clean, then they are done. If there is batter on it, then bake for another 10 minutes.

 236 kcal
 20.4 fat
 6.3 carbs
 3.6 fibre
 2.7 net
 6.4 protein

Chocolate Chip Muffins

Serves: 6

MUFFIN:

- 1/3 cup (40g) coconut flour
- 1 1/2 tsp baking powder
- 1/4 cup (50g) sugar substitute
- 3 tbsp coconut oil
- 3 eggs
- 1/2 cup (125ml) cream
- 1/2 cup (70g) sugar free chocolate chips

1. Mix the dry ingredients together in a bowl.
2. Add in the coconut oil and eggs and mix thoroughly.
3. Slowly pour in the cream as you stir the mix.
4. Spoon the batter into 6 lined muffin tins.
5. Bake at 350°F / 176° C for 30-40 minutes..

**At 30 minutes in, stick a toothpick into the middle of a muffin and if it comes out clean, then they are done. If there is batter on it, then bake for another 10 minutes.

 278 kcal
 23.4 fat
 4.7 carbs
 1.7 fibre
 3 net
 5.5 protein

Blueberry Muffins

Serves: 6

MUFFIN:

- 1/3 cup (40g) coconut flour
- 1/4 cup (50g) sugar substitute
- 1 tsp baking powder
- 3 tbsp coconut oil (melted), olive oil or melted butter
- 3 eggs
- 1 package (125g) blueberries

1. Mix the dry ingredients together in a bowl.
2. Add in the coconut oil, eggs and blueberry.
3. Mix thoroughly.
4. Spoon the batter into 6 lined muffin tins.
5. Bake at 350°F / 176° C for 30-40 minutes..

**At 30 minutes in, stick a toothpick into the middle of a muffin and if it comes out clean, then they are done. If there is batter on it, then bake for another 10 minutes.

 128 kcal
 10.1 fat
 5.8 carbs
 2.2 fibre
 3.6 net
 4 protein

Banana Chocolate Chip Muffins

Serves: 6

MUFFIN:

- 1/2 cup (70g) butter – melted
- 1/4 cup (50g) sugar substitute
- 1 egg
- 1 cup (100g) almond flour
- 1 tsp banana flavouring
- 1/2 tsp vanilla extract
- 1/2 sugar free chocolate bar (approx 35g) chips or shaved
- 1/2 tsp baking powder

1. Whisk the butter and sugar substitute together in a mixing bowl.
2. Add in the egg, flavours and extract.
3. Pour in the almond flour & baking powder and whisk until thoroughly mixed.
4. Stir in the chocolate chips/flakes.
5. Spoon the batter into a lined muffin tin.
6. Bake at 350°F / 175°C for roughly 25 minutes.

**At 30 minutes in, stick a toothpick into the middle of a muffin and if it comes out clean, then they are done. If there is batter on it, then bake for another 10 minutes.

 285 kcal
 27.9 fat
 5.2 carbs
 2 fibre
 3.2 net
 5.7 protein

Banana Chocolate Chip Bread

Serves: 14

INGREDIENTS:

- 1/2 cup (118ml) heavy cream
- 3 eggs
- 1/3 cup (75g) melted butter
- 1 tbsp banana extract
- 1/4 cup (50g) sugar substitute
- 2 cups (200g) almond flour
- 1 tsp baking powder
- 2/3 cup (100g) sugar free chocolate chips

1. Place all the ingredients into a mixing bowl.
2. Whisk together.
3. Pour the batter into a bread tin lined with parchment paper.
4. Bake at 350°F / 175°C for 45 minutes.

 224 kcal
 19.7 fat
 10.1 carbs
 2.4 fibre
 2.7 net
 5.7 protein

Almond Sweet Bread

Serves: 14

INGREDIENTS:

- 2 1/4 cups (225g) almond flour
- 1/2 cup (100g) butter
- 1/2 cup (100g) sugar substitute
- 1/2 cup (118ml) heavy cream
- 1/2 tsp xanthan gum
- 1 tsp baking powder
- 1/4 tsp ginger powder (optional)
- 1/4 tsp ground star anise (optional)
- 2 tbsp ground flaxseed
- 2 eggs

1. In a pot over medium heat, melt the butter.
2. Stir in the sugar substitute and heavy cream
3. Stir frequently until the sugar substitute has dissolved.
4. Take off heat and let it cool to room temperature.
5. In a mixing bowl, whisk together the dry ingredients.
6. Pour the cooled butter/cream mix, and whisk in the two eggs.
7. Pour into a bread tin lined with parchment paper.
8. Bake at 350°F/175°C for approximately 45-50 minutes.

206 kcal | 19.8 fat | 4.5 carbs | 2.2 fibre | 2.3 net | 5.2 protein

Cinnamon Bread

Serves: 14

BREAD:
- 1/2 cup (118ml) heavy cream
- 3 eggs
- 1/3 cup (75g) melted butter
- 1 tsp vanilla extract
- 1 tbsp caramel flavouring
- 1 tbsp toffee flavouring
- 2 cups (200g) almond flour
- 1 tsp baking powder
- 1/4 cup (50g) sugar substitute
- 1/4 tsp xanthan gum
- 1 tbsp cinnamon
- 1/2 tsp nutmeg
- 1/2 tsp ginger

FILLING:
- 1/2 cup (115g) cream cheese
- 1 tsp vanilla
- 1/8th cup (25g) sugar substitute

1. In a mixing bowl, whisk all the bread ingredients together.
2. In a separate mixing bowl, stir together the cream cheese, sugar substitute and vanilla.
3. Pour half the bread batter into a bread tin lined with parchment paper.
4. Spoon or pipe the cream cheese on top of the bread batter. Leave some room around the edges so that the cream cheese won't leak out when taken out of the tin.
5. Pour the rest of the bread batter on top of the cream cheese
6. Bake at 350°F/175°C for 45 minutes.

 206 kcal
 19.4 fat
 4.7 carbs
 2 fibre
 2.7 net
 5.5 protein

Hawaiian Sweet Bread

Serves: 10

BREAD:

- 2 cups (200g) almond flour
- 1 1/2 cups (100g) whey protein isolate
- 1/2 cup (100g) sugar substitute
- 3 tsp baking powder
- 2 tsp xanthan gum
- 1 cup (236ml) warm water
- 1 tsp pineapple flavour
- 1/2 tsp salt

1. In a bowl, whisk together the almond flour, protein, xanthan gum, baking powder, sugar substitute and salt.
2. Measure out the warm water and stir in the pineapple flavouring.
3. Pour the pineapple water into the flour and mix thoroughly with a spoon.
4. With wet hands, take a handful of the dough and form a ball.
5. Place the dough balls into the deep dish that is greased or lined with parchment paper.
6. Use wet fingers to smooth the tops of the balls.
7. Bake at 375°F / 175°C for 30 minutes.

| 172 kcal | 11.3 fat | 6.6 carbs | 3.8 fibre | 2.8 net | 13.8 protein |

Bread Pudding

Serves: 8

BREAD:

- 1/2 cup (100g) melted butter
- 1/2 cup (118ml) water
- 2 eggs
- 1 tbsp vanilla
- 1/4 cup (50g) sugar substitute
- 2 cups (200g) almond flour
- 1 tsp baking powder

PUDDING:

- 1 cup (250ml) heavy cream
- 2 eggs
- 1/4 cup (50g) sugar substitute
- 1 tbsp vanilla
- 2 tbsp melted butter
- 1 tsp cinnamon
- 1/2 tsp nutmeg

1. In a mixing bowl, stir together the melted butter, eggs, water, vanilla and sugar substitute.
2. Whisk in the almond flour and baking powder.
3. Pour into a greased or lined loaf tin.
4. Bake at 350°F/175°C for approximately 45 minutes.
5. In another mixing bowl, whisk together the pudding ingredients.
6. Once the loaf has cooled, either cut or tear it into chunks and place the chunks into a casserole dish.
7. Pour the pudding mixture onto the bread.
8. Bake at 350°F/175°C for 45 minutes.
9. Once done, top with extra cinnamon and a sprinkling of sugar substitute!

 451 kcal
 44.6 fat
 7 carbs
 3 fibre
 4 net
 9.9 protein

Lemon Loaf (Starbucks Copycat!)

Serves: 14

INGREDIENTS:

- 4 tbsp sour cream
- 1 tsp lemon extract
- 2 squeezes (2 tbsp) lemon juice
- 1/4 cup (50g) butter - melted
- 1/3 cup (67g) sugar substitute
- 1 tsp lemon zest
- 2 eggs
- 2 cups (200g) almond flour
- 1 tsp baking powder
- 1 tsp poppy seeds

1. In a large mixing bowl, whisk together all the loaf ingredients.

2. Pour the mixture into a bread tin that is lined with parchment paper.

3. Bake at 350°F / 175°C for 30 minutes or until a toothpick comes out clean.

*Lemon extract is crucial to get the similar taste to Starbucks lemon loaf.

 139 kcal
 12.7 fat
 3.9 carbs
 1.8 fibre
 2,1 net
 4.5 protein

contents.

CHOCOLATE CHIP COOKIES	88
GINGERBREAD COOKIES	91
PEANUT BUTTER COOKIES	92
PAN DE POLVO	95
SNICKERDOODLE	96
OREOS	99
CHOCOLATE COOKIES	100
RED VELVET COOKIES	103
LEMON COOKIES	104
SNOWBALL COOKIES	107

Chocolate Chip Cookies

Serves: 18

COOKIE:

- 3/4 cup (150g) butter – room temperature
- 1/2 cup (100g) sugar substitute
- 1 tsp vanilla extract
- 2 cups (200g) almond flour
- 1/2 tsp baking soda
- 1/4 tsp xanthan gum
- 2/3 cup (100g) sugar free chocolate chips
- Egg

1. In a large mixing bowl, use a stand mixer or spatula to cream the butter, sugar substitute and vanilla together.
2. Crack in the egg and mix again.
3. Pour in the almond flour, baking powder and xanthan gum.
4. Mix thoroughly. Make sure that the dough is very well mixed and that there are no clumps of butter in the dough.
5. Stir in the chocolate chips.
6. Use the hands to roll the dough into balls. (If you want flat cookies, use the palm of the hands to press the ball of dough flatter)
7. Place the cookies on a cookie sheet lined with parchment paper.
8. Bake at 350°F / 175°C for 15-20 minutes or until the top is golden brown.

 152 kcal
 14.2 fat
 3.1 carbs
 1.5 fibre
 1.6 net
 3.1 protein

Gingerbread Cookies

Serves: 15

COOKIE:

- 3 tbsp (approx 50g) room temperature butter
- 3 tbsp brown sugar substitute
- 1 cup (100g) almond flour
- 1 tbsp vanilla extract
- 1/2 tbsp ginger powder
- 1 tsp cinnamon
- 1 tsp ground cloves
- 1 tsp nutmeg
- 1/2 tsp salt

1. In a large mixing bowl, use a hand or stand mixer to whip together the butter, salt, sugar substitute and vanilla.
2. Add in the almond flour and spices.
3. Mix together with the hands and knead it! It will eventually form a nice big lump of dough.
4. Roll out the dough and cut into shapes.
5. Bake at 350°F/175°C for 10 minutes.

55 kcal | 5.1 fat | 1.7 carbs | 0.8 fibre | 0.9 net | 1.4 protein

Peanut Butter Cookies

Serves: 14

COOKIE:

- 4 tbsp (50g) butter – room temp
- 3 tbsp sugar substitute
- 3 tbsp peanut butter (no sugar added)
- 1 tsp vanilla
- 1 cup (100g) almond flour

1. In a mixing bowl, use a spatula to cream the butter, sugar substitute, vanilla and peanut butter together. Make sure it is very well mixed and no clumps of butter remain.
2. Pour in the almond flour and continue to mix.
3. Knead with the hands until a dough forms.
4. Roll into a log and cut into 1-inch circles.
5. Place the cookies on a baking sheet lined with parchment paper.
6. Cook at 350°F/175°C for 10 minutes.

91 kcal | 9.2 fat | 2.1 carbs | 1 fibre | 1.1 net | 2.7 protein

Pan de Polvo | Mexican Shortbread

Serves: 20

COOKIE:

- 3/4 cup (150g) butter – room temperature
- 2 cups (200g) almond flour
- 1 1/2 cups (354ml) boiling water
- 1 tsp baking powder
- 1/4 tsp xanthan gum
- 1 stick cinnamon
- 1 bag of anise tea (or 2 tsp seeds)
- 5 tbsp sugar substitute
- 1 tsp cinnamon

1. Place the cinnamon stick, anise and boiling water into a cup and cool to room temperature.
2. Place the butter, almond flour, baking powder and xanthan gum in a mixing bowl.
3. Mix the butter and almond flour until it becomes a soft graham cracker type mix.
4. Slowly pour in 1/4 cup (60ml) of the cooled cinnamon/anise water into the dough.
5. Use the hands to knead the almond flour into a smooth dough.
6. Roll into a log approximately 20 inches in length.
7. Wrap in cling wrap and cool for 30 minutes.
8. Cut into 20 circular cookies.
9. Place on a cookie sheet lined with parchment paper and bake for 10-12 minutes at 350°F / 175°C
10. Whisk together the sugar substitute and cinnamon and sprinkle on top of the baked cookies.

125 kcal | 12.5 fat | 2.5 carbs | 1.3 fibre | 1.2 net | 2.5 protein

Snickerdoodle Cookies

Serves: 18

COOKIE:

- 1/2 cup (100g) butter – room temperature
- 1/4 cup (50g) sugar substitute
- 1/8th cup (25g) extra sugar substitute (for coating)
- 1 tsp vanilla
- 1 egg
- 1 1/2 cups (150g) almond flour
- 3/4 tsp baking powder
- 1 tbsp cinnamon

1. In a mixing bowl, cream together the butter and 1/4 cup sugar substitute.
2. Once blended well, add in the egg and vanilla and mix again.
3. Pour in the almond flour and baking powder and whisk together. Make sure that it is all mixed and that there are no clumps of butter in the dough.
4. In a separate bowl, mix together the cinnamon and 1/8th cup of sugar substitute.
5. Take a small scoop of the dough and form a ball with the hands.
6. Roll the dough balls into the cinnamon/sugar mix, coating the entire cookie.
7. Place on a cookie sheet lined with parchment paper and bake at 375°F/190°C for 12 minutes.

 104 kcal
 10 fat
 2,2 carbs
 1.1 fibre
 1.1 net
 2.4 protein

Oreos

Serves: 15

COOKIE:

- 3 tbsp (50g) room temperature butter
- 3 tbsp powdered sugar substitute
- 1 tsp vanilla
- 1 cup (100g) almond flour
- 3 tbsp dark cocoa powder

FILLING:

- 1/4 cup (50g) shortening (or butter)
- 3 tbsp (50g) butter - room temperature
- 3/4 cup (95g) powdered sugar substitute
- 1 tsp vanilla
- 1 tsp heavy cream

1. Use a stand or hand mixer to thoroughly mix the butter, sugar substitute and vanilla.
2. Pour in the almond flour and the scoops of cocoa powder. Continue to mix until a dough forms.
3. Roll out the dough between two pieces of parchment paper.
4. Use a cookie cutter to cut an even number of cookies.
5. Bake the cookies for 10 minutes at 350°F/175°C.
6. Place the shortening, butter, heavy cream, sugar substitute and flavouring into a mixing bowl.
7. Use a hand mixer or spatula to mix the ingredients together until nice and fluffy.
8. Place a dollop of the cream between two cookies and enjoy!

 116 kcal
 11.6 fat
 2,2 carbs
 1.2 fibre
 1 net
 1.7 protein

Chocolate Cookies

Serves: 15

COOKIE:

- 1/2 cup (100g) butter - room temp
- 4 tbsp sugar substitute
- 1 tsp vanilla
- 1 tbsp cocoa powder
- 1 egg
- 1 1/2 cups (150g) almond flour
- 1/2 tsp xanthan gum
- 1/2 tsp baking soda

1. In a mixing bowl, cream together the butter, vanilla, sugar substitute and cocoa powder. Make sure it is mixed thoroughly.
2. Pour in the almond flour, xanthan gum and baking soda. Use a spoon to stir it all together. It will eventually turn into a coarse graham cracker like consistency.
3. Add in the egg and whisk.
4. Cool the dough in the fridge for half an hour.
5. Scoop tablespoon sized amounts of dough onto a cookie sheet lined with parchment paper.
6. Use wet hands to smooth and flatten the dough balls.
7. Bake at 350°F / 175°C for 15 minutes.

kcal	fat	carbs	fibre	net	protein
126	12.1	3.1	1.8	1.5	3

Red Velvet Cookies

Serves: 15

COOKIE:

- 1/2 cup (100g) butter - room temp
- 4 tbsp sugar substitute
- 1 tsp vanilla
- 1 tbsp cocoa powder
- 1 egg
- 1 1/2 cups (150g) almond flour
- 1/2 tsp xanthan gum
- 1/2 tsp baking soda
- Red food colouring

TOPPING:

- 4 tbsp cream cheese
- 1 tsp vanilla
- 2 tbsp powdered sugar substitute
- 1 1/2 tbsp water

1. In a mixing bowl, cream together the butter, vanilla, sugar substitute, food colouring and cocoa powder.
2. Mix in the almond flour, xanthan gum and baking soda. It will eventually turn into a coarse graham cracker like consistency.
3. Add in the egg and whisk.
4. Cool the dough in the fridge for half an hour.
5. Scoop tablespoon sized amounts of dough onto a cookie sheet lined with parchment paper.
6. Use wet hands to smooth and flatten the dough balls.
7. Bake at 350°F / 175°C for 15 minutes.
8. Stir together the powdered sugar substitute, vanilla, cream cheese and water.
9. Pipe the icing onto the top of the cooled cookies and enjoy!

 139 kcal
 13.4 fat
 3.3 carbs
 1.8 fibre
 1.5 net
 3.2 protein

Lemon Cookies

Serves: 15

COOKIE:

- 1/2 cup (100g) butter - room temperature
- 1 tbsp lemon zest (1 lemon)
- 1/3 cup (67g) sugar substitute
- 1 tsp lemon extract
- 2 squeezes - lemon juice (2 tbsp)
- 1 egg
- 1 1/2 cup (150g) almond flour
- 1 tsp baking soda
- 1/2 tsp xanthan gum

1. In a large mixing bowl, use a hand or stand mixer to whip together the butter, sugar substitute, lemon zest, extract and juice.
2. Mix until nice and creamy with no major chunks of butter.
3. Crack in the egg and mix thoroughly again.
4. Pour in the almond flour, baking soda and xanthan gum and mix until a dough forms.
5. Place the bowl in the fridge for a minimum of 30 minutes.
6. Once chilled, take a small scoop of the dough and use the hands to roll into a ball.
7. Place the dough cookies onto a cookie sheet lined with parchment paper.
8. Bake at 350°F/175°C for 10 minutes or until the edges begin to turn brown.

 124 kcal
 12.1 fat
 2.7 carbs
 1.4 fibre
 1.3 net
 2.9 protein

Snowball Cookies

Serves: 18

INGREDIENTS:

- 3/4 cup (150g) butter - room temperature
- 2 cups (200g) almond flour
- 1/2 cup (100g) sugar substitute
- 1 tsp xanthan gum
- 1 tsp baking powder
- 1/2 cup (50g) pecans - chopped
- powdered sugar substitute for rolling

1. In a mixing bowl, use a hand or stand mixer to beat the butter, sugar substitute and vanilla until smooth.
2. Slowly mix in the almond flour, xanthan gum and baking powder. Once it's thoroughly mixed together, it should resemble coarse graham crackers with butter.
3. Use the hands to knead it together. Make sure there are no clumps of butter in the dough.
4. Freeze for 15 minutes
5. Roll the dough into 18 cookie balls
6. Bake the cookies at 350°F / 175°C for 15-20 minutes.
7. Once the cookies have cooled, roll them in confectioners sugar substitute.

160 kcal | 16.1 fat | 3.1 carbs | 1.6 fibre | 1.5 net | 3 protein

more sweets & treats

contents.

CHOCOLATE PUDDING	110
CREME BRULEE	113
FLAN	114
CONDENSED MILK	117
VEGAN CONDENSED MILK	118
NANAIMO BARS	121
BUTTER TARTS	122
LEMON BARS	125
CINNAMON BUNS	126
MOONPIES	129
PECAN COBBLER	130
WHITE CHOCOLATE	133
THE PERFECT MUG CAKE	134

Eggless Chocolate Pudding

Serves: 4

INGREDIENTS:

- 1/2 cup (43g) unsweetened cocoa
- 1/2 cup (100g) sugar substitute
- 1/2 tsp xantham gum
- 1 1/2 cups (354ml) heavy whipping cream

1. In a small sauce pan, mix together the dry ingredients.
2. Slowly whisk in the whipping cream.
3. Turn the burner on to medium and bring the pudding to a boil.. stir constantly.
4. It will start to thicken pretty much immediately.
5. Once you can dip a spoon into the pudding and it comes out covered in pudding, you're done!

381 kcal | 31 fat | 6.5 carbs | 4.3 fibre | 2.2 net | 2.1 protein

Creme Brûlée

Serves: 3

INGREDIENTS:

- 3 egg yolks
- 1 cup (236ml) cream
- 1/4 cup (50g) sugar substitute
- 1 tsp vanilla
- boiling water
- 3 tsp extra sugar substitute

1. Mix together the 1/4 cup sugar substitute, cream and vanilla until the sugar sub has dissolved.
2. Beat the egg yolks with a whisk.
3. Slowly add the cream mix into the yolks as you whisk.
4. Pour it into 3 ramekins.
5. Place the ramekins on a casserole dish and fill the dish with 2-3 inches of boiling water.
6. Bake at 350 for 30-40 minutes. It'll be done once the custard is firm on the outside but jiggly in the centre. Let it cool.
7. Top the ramekins with 1 tsp sugar substitute and use a torch to caramelize.
8. Cool and serve!

 205 kcal
 19.3 fat
 2.3 carbs
 0 fibre
 2.3 net
 3.5 protein

Flan

Serves: 4

CARAMEL:

- 4 tbsp erythritol
- 1/4 cup (60ml) water
- 1 tbsp butter

PUDDING:

- 1 cup (250ml) heavy cream
- 1/4 cup (50g) sugar substitute
- 1 tsp vanilla
- 2 whole eggs
- 1 egg yolk

1. In a deep pan, heat up the erythritol and water on medium-low.
2. Bring it to a simmer before adding in the butter.
3. Stir occasionally until it becomes a dark amber colour.
4. Scoop the caramel into three ramekins. Let it sit and cool.
5. In a mixing bowl, whisk together the eggs and egg yolk
6. Pour in the cream, 1/4 cup of erythritol and vanilla.
7. Whisk until the sugar substitute has dissolved.
8. Pour the mixture into the ramekins on top of the caramel.
9. Place the ramekins on a casserole dish and fill the dish with 2-3 inches of boiling water.
10. Bake at 350 for 30-40 minutes.

283 kcal | 27.6 fat | 2.3 carbs | 0 fibre | 2.3 net | 5.7 protein

Condensed 'Milk' (Cream)

*nutritional information is per tbsp

INGREDIENTS:

- 2 cups (500ml) heavy cream
- 4 tbsp confectioners sugar substitute
- 2 tbsp butter
- 1 tsp vanilla

1. In a pan, melt the butter on medium-high heat.
2. Scoop in the sugar substitute and vanilla. Stir together.
3. Pour in the heavy cream.
4. Stir continuously and bring to a boil.
5. Once the cream starts to boil, turn down the heat to medium-low, continue stirring.
6. Let the cream simmer until it has reduced by HALF. Stir frequently so it does not burn to the pan.
7. When the cream is done, it should be a pale yellow colour and the consistency of pudding.

 115 kcal
 12.4 fat
 0.8 carbs
 0 fibre
 0.8 net
 0.6 protein

Vegan Condensed 'Milk'

*nutritional information is per tbsp

INGREDIENTS:

- 1 can (400ml) coconut milk
- 4 tbsp confectioners sugar substitute

1. In a pan, whisk together the coconut milk and sugar substitute.
2. Stir continuously and bring the to a boil.
3. Once the milk starts to boil, turn down the heat to medium-low, continue stirring.
4. Let the milk simmer until it has reduced by HALF. Stir frequently so it does not burn to the pan.
5. When the milk is done, it should be a pale yellow colour and the consistency of pudding.

 44 kcal
 4.4 fat
 0.9 carbs
 0 fibre
 0.9 net
 0.3 protein

Nanaimo Bars

Serves: 25
*Instructions start with ingredients from layer 1

1st LAYER:
- 1/2 cup (100g) butter
- 1/4 cup (50g) sugar substitute
- 1 egg – beaten
- 5 tbsp cocoa
- 1 cup (100g) almond flour
- 1 cup (75g) unsweetened coconut

2nd LAYER:
- 1/2 cup (100g) butter
- 2 tbsp custard powder
- 1 cup (140g) powdered sugar substitute
- 2 tbsp + 2 tsp heavy cream

3rd LAYER:
- 2 tbsp butter
- 4oz unsweetened chocolate
- 1 tbsp sugar substitute

1. Melt butter, sugar and cocoa together on medium-low heat.
2. Slowly stir in the egg and whisk until it starts to thicken.
3. Take off heat and stir in almond flour and coconut.
4. Spread the almond coconut dough on the bottom of a brownie or casserole dish.
5. In a mixing bowl, whip together the butter, custard powder, sugar substitute and cream.
6. Once fluffy, spread over the top of the 1st layer.
7. Melt the butter over low heat.
8. Add in the chocolate and sugar substitute, stirring until they dissolve.
9. Take off heat and cool for 5 minutes.
10. Pour on top of the 2nd layer.
11. Refrigerate for 2-4 hours.

 189 kcal
 15.4 fat
 5.2 carbs
 2.3 fibre
 2.9 net
 2.3 protein

Butter Tarts

Serves: 8

CRUST:
- 3/4 cup (90g) coconut flour
- 1/2 cup (100g) butter – melted
- 2 eggs
- 3 tbsp sugar substitute

FILLING:
- 2 eggs
- 1/3 cup (50g) softened butter
- 1 cup (175g) packed brown sugar substitute
- 1 tsp vanilla
- 4 tbsp heavy cream

1. For the crust, stir together the coconut flour, eggs, sugar substitute and melted butter.
2. Scoop some of the crust and line the inside of a greased muffin tin.
3. In a pot, whisk together the filling ingredients.
4. Place pot on medium heat and stir constantly otherwise it will burn.
5. Continue to whisk until the butter has melted.
6. Pour the filling into the crust lined muffin tins.
7. Bake at 350°F / 175°C for 15-20 minutes.
8. You will know it's done when it turns a pale golden colour.

210 kcal | 18.3 fat | 6.4 carbs | 3.8 fibre | 2.6 net | 4.9 protein

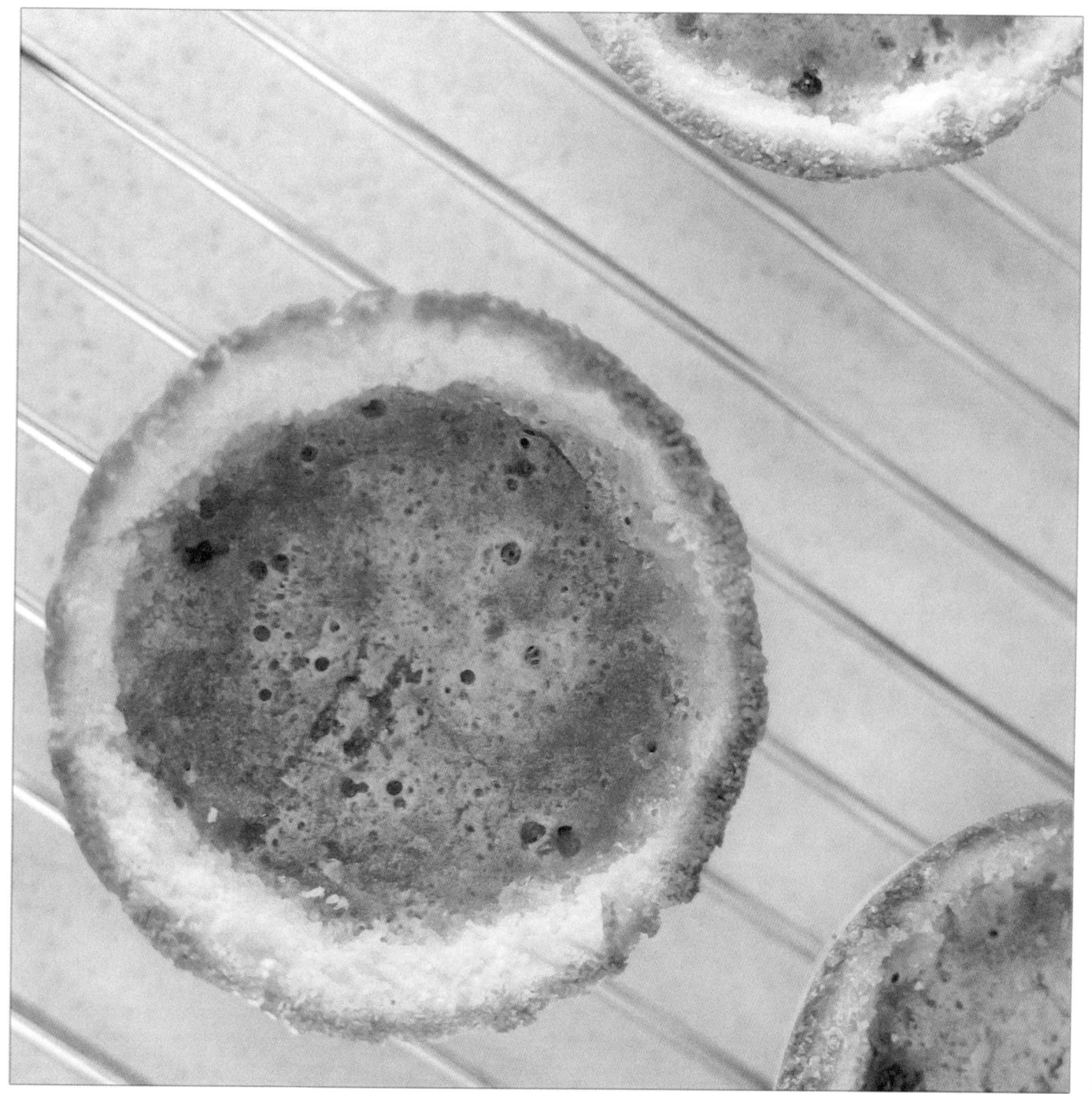

Lemon Bars

Serves: 12

CRUST:
- 1 ½ cups (150g) almond flour
- 1/4 cup (50g) sugar substitute
- ¾ cup (165g) butter – room temp

FILLING:
- 3 eggs
- 1 egg yolk
- 1/2 cup (100g) sugar substitute
- ½ cup (118ml) lemon juice
- 1 tablespoon lemon zest
- ¼ cup (25g) almond flour

1. For the crust, place all the crust ingredients into a bowl and use the hands to knead it together thoroughly.
2. Transfer the dough to a 9×9 pan and use the hands to make a crust that lines the bottom of the pan.
3. Bake at 325°F/160°C for 20 minutes or until the crust is a nice golden brown.
4. Place all the ingredients for the filling into a bowl and whisk together.
5. Pour the lemon filling onto the crust and put it back in the oven.
6. Bake at the same temperature for 25 minutes.
7. Take out and cool to room temperature before refrigerating for a minimum of 4 hours.

 220 kcal
 21,3 fat
 4.4 carbs
 1.9 fibre
 2.5 net
 5.5 protein

Cinnamon Buns

Serves: 6

BUNS:
- 1 1/2 cups (170g) mozzarella cheese
- 3/4 cup (85g) almond flour
- 2 tbsp cream cheese
- 2 tbsp sugar substitute
- 1/2 tsp baking powder
- 1 tsp cinnamon
- 1 tsp vanilla
- 1 egg

FILLING:
- 1/4 cup (50g) butter – melted
- 1/4 cup (50g) white sugar substitute
- 1/4 cup (40g) brown sugar substitute
- 1 tbsp cinnamon

GLAZE
- 1/3 cup (90g) cream cheese- room temp
- 1 1/2 tbsp sugar substitute
- 1 tsp vanilla
- 1 tbsp heavy cream

1. Microwave or double boil the mozzarella and cream cheese until it has melted.
2. Mix in the almond flour, cinnamon, sugar substitute, baking powder, egg and vanilla.
3. Mix until a dough forms.
4. Roll the dough flat. Place the dough between two pieces of parchment paper to prevent sticking.
5. Whisk together the filling ingredients.
6. Pour the filling onto the dough and use a spatula to spread it around.
7. Roll the dough together to form a long roll - like a rolled up carpet.
8. Cut into 6 pieces and place in a greased or parchment line muffin tin.
9. Bake at 350°F/175°C for 25 minutes.
10. Whisk the cream cheese, sugar substitute, vanilla and heavy cream into a bowl.
11. Use a spoon or pipe the icing mixture over the finished buns.

 304 kcal
 27 fat
 5.1 carbs
 1.7 fibre
 3.4 net
 11.2 protein

Moonpies

Serves: 5

CAKE:
- 1/4 cup (50g) sour cream
- 1/4 cup (50g) butter – melted
- 1 egg
- 1/4 cup (59ml) heavy cream
- 1 cup (100g) almond flour
- 1/2 tsp baking powder
- 3 tbsp cocoa powder
- 1/4 cup (50g) sugar substitute

FILLING:
- 3/4 cup (170g) mascarpone cheese
- 1 tsp vanilla
- 1/4 cup (50g) sugar substitute

GANACHE
- 1 sugar free, keto chocolate bar
- 3 tbsp heavy cream

1. In a small mixing bowl, whisk together the filling ingredients.
2. Cover and chill in the fridge.
3. In a larger mixing bowl, stir together all the cake ingredients
4. Spread a small (1/4 cup) scoop of the batter into a non-stick 12cm (5-inch) spring form pan.
5. Either using a spoon, or a piping bag, place a layer of the mascarpone cream on top of the batter.
6. Place another scoop of batter on top of the cream and spread it around, effectively covering all the cream.
7. Put the cake(s) in the oven at 350°F/175°C for 20 minutes.
8. Place the keto chocolate bar & cream in a microwavable dish and microwave until the chocolate has melted.
9. Pour onto the cooled cakes and spread around with a spatula.
10. Cool for minimum 1 hour.

 193 kcal
 18.7 fat
 5.5 carbs
 2 fibre
 3.5 net
 4.9 protein

Pecan Cobbler

Serves: 10

BATTER:

- 6 tbsp (75g) butter
- 1 1/2 cups (150g) pecans – chopped
- 1 1/2 cups (150g) almond flour
- 1/2 tsp baking powder
- salt
- 1 tbsp cinnamon
- 1/2 cup (100g) erythritol
- 1 cup (250ml) heavy cream
- 1 tbsp vanilla

TOPPING

- 1/2 cup (90g) brown sugar substitute
- 1/8th (25g) sugar substitute
- 1 cup (236ml) boiling water

1. Preheat the oven to 350°F/175°C.
2. Place the butter in a 9×13 inch casserole dish and put in the oven to melt.
3. In a mixing bowl, whisk together the almond flour, erythritol, baking powder, vanilla and heavy cream. Set aside.
4. Once the butter is melted, line the casserole dish with chopped pecans..
5. Pour the almond flour batter on top of the pecans. Spread it around evenly
6. For the topping, whisk together both sugar substitutes and sprinkle it on top of the batter.
7. Pour the boiling water on top of the batter but do not mix.
8. Bake for 70-90 minutes until the water has dissolved..

NOTE: Check at 45 minutes, then every 10 minutes after. Take out if you smell burning!!

 342 kcal
 34.9 fat
 6.6 carbs
 3.4 fibre
 3.2 net
 5.5 protein

White Chocolate

*Nutrtitional Information is for entire chocolate bar

INGREDIENTS:

- 8oz Cacao butter
- 4-5 tbsp powdered sugar substitute
- Any toppings you want, such as cayenne pepper, almonds etc.

1. Heat up the cacao butter using a double boiler.

2. Once the cacao butter has melted and is a nice yellow colour, add in the sugar substitute and whisk until it is all mixed together.

3. Pour the mix into molds or a parchment paper lined baking sheet or into individual molds.

4. Freeze or refrigerate until the chocolate is a nice white colour. Approx 2-3 hours.

2000 kcal | 224 fat | 0 carbs | 0 fibre | 0 net | 0 protein

Perfect 1-Minute Chocolate Cake

Serves: 1

INGREDIENTS:

- 3 tbsp almond flour
- 1/2 tsp baking powder
- 1 tsp vanilla extract
- 1 large egg yolk
- 1/2 tbsp sour cream
- 1 tbsp heavy cream
- 1 tbsp cocoa powder
- 1 tbsp sugar substitute

1. In a mug, whisk together the dry ingredients.
2. Add in the egg yolk, sour cream, heavy cream and flavourings.
3. Whisk together again.
4. Place in the microwave and cook for 90 seconds
5. Take out and enjoy!

NOTE: The 90 seconds is based on a medium-high 700w microwave. If you have a 1000w microwave, try microwaving for 50-60 seconds Check at 30s, 60s. Look for a cake like texture, if it's spongy and rubbery, it's overcooked.

251 kcal | 22.5 fat | 9 carbs | 4.2 fibre | 4.8 net | 8.7 protein

Follow.

▶ youtube.com/hungryelephant

◉ instagram.com/hungryelephant

Subscribe.

facebook.com/ahungryelephant

twitter.com/ahungryelephant

Thank

You

Made in the USA
Las Vegas, NV
20 April 2022